Safe Behind a Mask

Contents

Mick Gowar

OXFORD

Introduction

Since ancient times people have worn masks to protect themselves.

In war

For thousands of years soldiers have worn masks in battle. These masks helped to keep them safe from enemy attack.

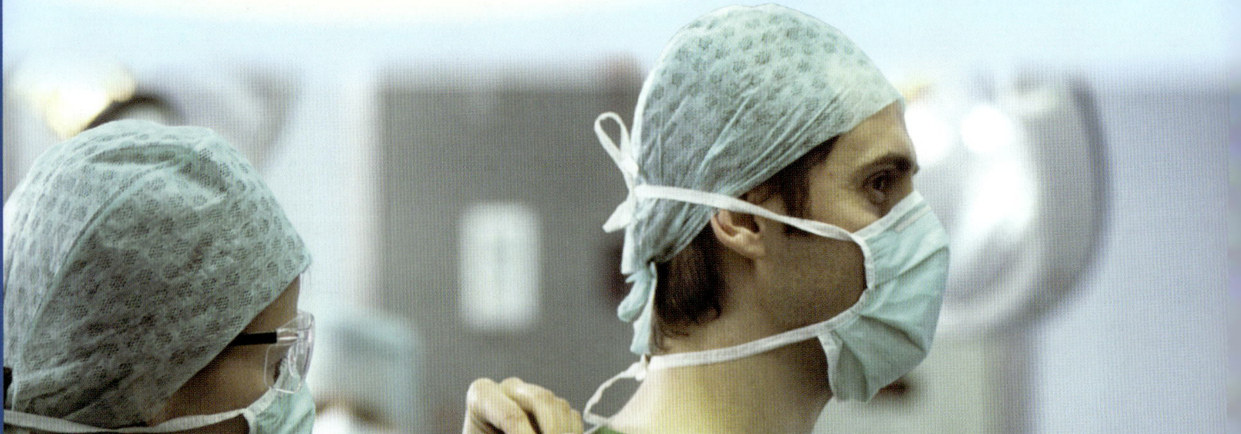

For health

Doctors and nurses wear masks to stop the spread of **diseases** when they're looking after sick people.

Other uses for masks

See page 17

See page 13

See page 18

See page 19

See page 21

Q Do you know why these people are wearing masks? What are they trying to protect themselves from?

Battle masks

Spartan warriors were once famous for being the bravest and fiercest soldiers in all Greece.

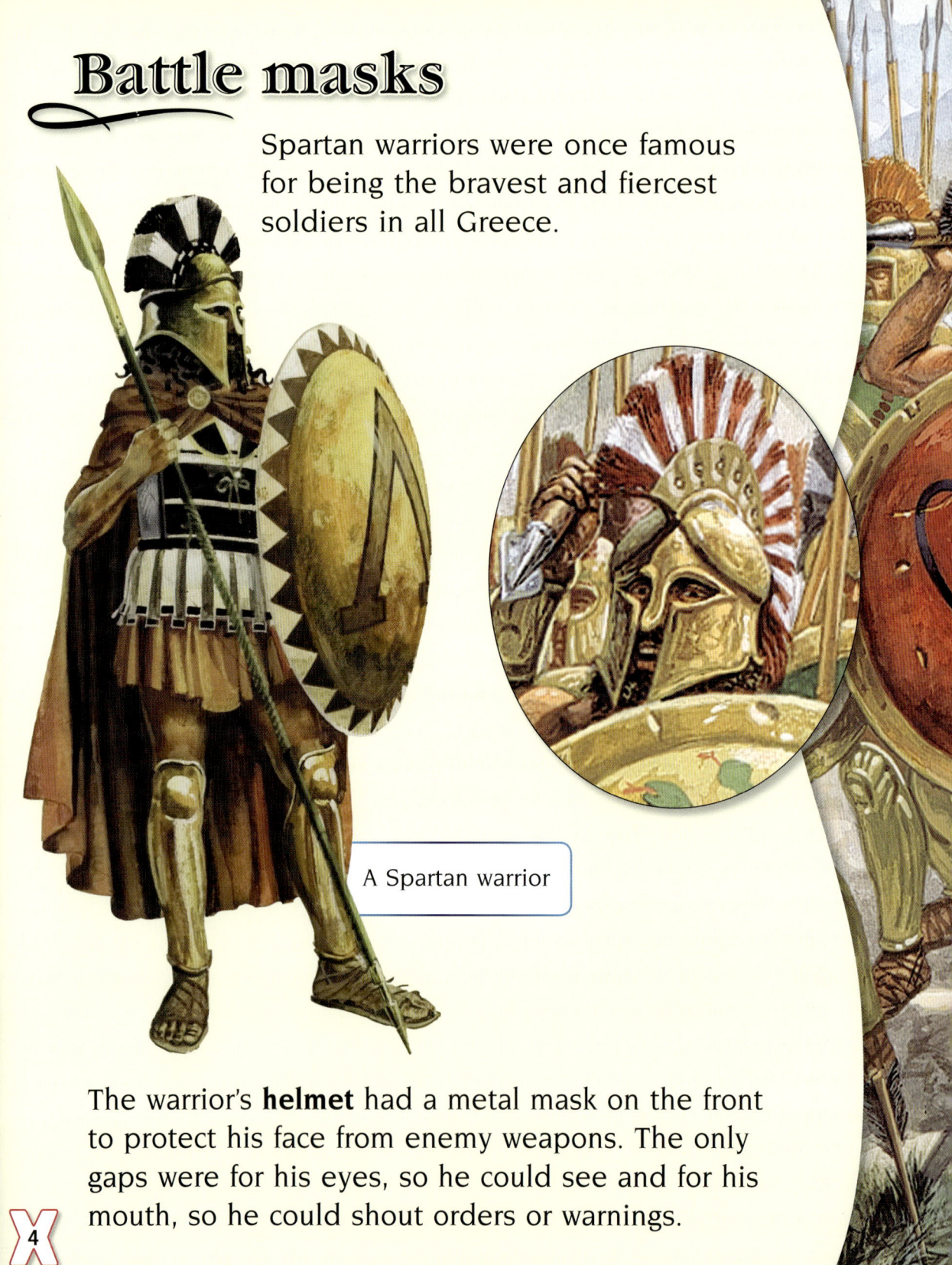

A Spartan warrior

The warrior's **helmet** had a metal mask on the front to protect his face from enemy weapons. The only gaps were for his eyes, so he could see and for his mouth, so he could shout orders or warnings.

Spartan warriors fought side by side. They formed a great wall of **shields**. From behind this wall they stabbed at their enemies with swords and spears.

Who's who?

Warriors from other Greek cities, like Athens, also wore helmets with masks.

When Spartans fought Athenians it was difficult to tell who was on your side and who was an enemy. So each soldier had a special **sign** painted on their shield to show who they were.

Shields

Medieval knights had **symbols** painted on their shields to show who they were and which family they belonged to. They also wore coats over their **armour** with their family symbols on them.

Q If you had to decorate a shield, what pictures would you choose to show who you are?

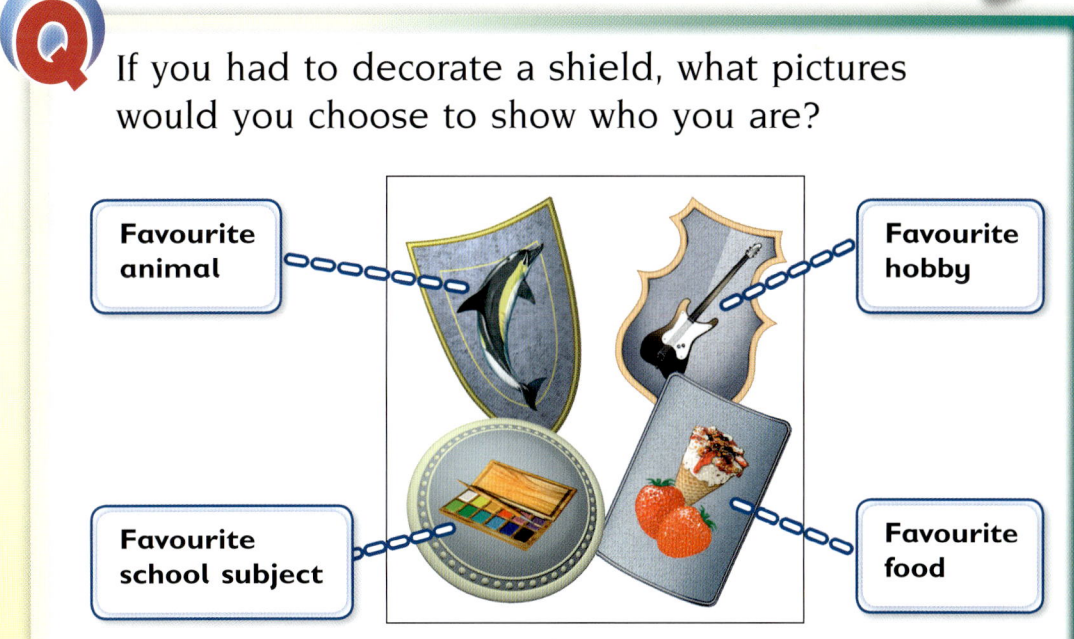

Favourite animal

Favourite hobby

Favourite school subject

Favourite food

Armour

The mask on a **knight's** helmet is called a **visor**. It was great protection but it was very hard to see through!

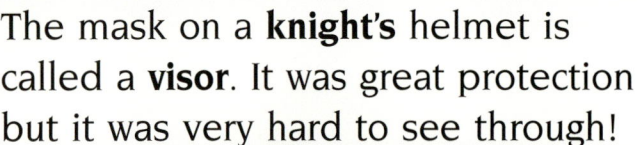

Visor

Armour was made for a knight and his horse. Both the knight and his horse had masks to protect their faces.

If a knight wasn't in danger, he could put his visor up to see where he was going. If his visor got stuck, he would be in great danger!

Henry VIII, King of England, had a new suit of armour and wanted to show it off. He organised a **jousting** contest. The first fight was between the King and the Duke of Suffolk.

The King began to gallop down the ground.
"The King is coming!" shouted the crowd.
"Where?" asked the Duke. "I can't see anything." He started galloping towards the King.
The King tried to lower his visor. It was stuck.
"Stop!" shouted the crowd.
But the Duke didn't hear him.

The Duke's spear smashed against the King's visor.
"The Duke tried to kill the King!" shouted the crowd.
"It's no one's fault but mine," laughed the King.

Gas masks

In modern wars everyone needs protection, not just soldiers. Nowadays planes can drop **bombs** onto towns and cities.

Sometimes these bombs aren't just meant to destroy buildings. Some bombs spread poisoned **gas** or deadly **germs**.

During the Second World War, everyone in Britain was given a gas mask in case the enemy dropped gas bombs. Even children were given gas masks. They had to carry them everywhere they went. Small children were given red and blue masks that were supposed to look like Mickey Mouse!

How a gas mask works

When the person wearing the mask breathes in, the air has to pass through thick **filters**. These filters block the poisoned gas and only let clean air through.

Clean air

Filters

Poisoned gas

The plague

In 1660, a terrible disease called the Black Death swept across London. It was caused by fleas.

Fleas drank the blood of sick rats. Then they bit people and **infected** them with germs from the rats.

People thought the **plague** was caused by bad smells in the air. Doctors who tried to cure the plague **victims** wore special masks and clothes to protect themselves against the bad air.

A mask with:
- goggles to protect the doctor's eyes
- beak filled with herbs to cover bad smells

thick gloves to protect the doctor's hands

coat covered in wax to keep out bad air

A plague doctor in his special clothes.

Medical masks

Today, we know much more about how diseases are really spread but doctors and nurses still wear masks.

Many diseases are caused by tiny living creatures called bacteria. Bacteria are so small they can be breathed in and spread by coughing and sneezing.

bacteria

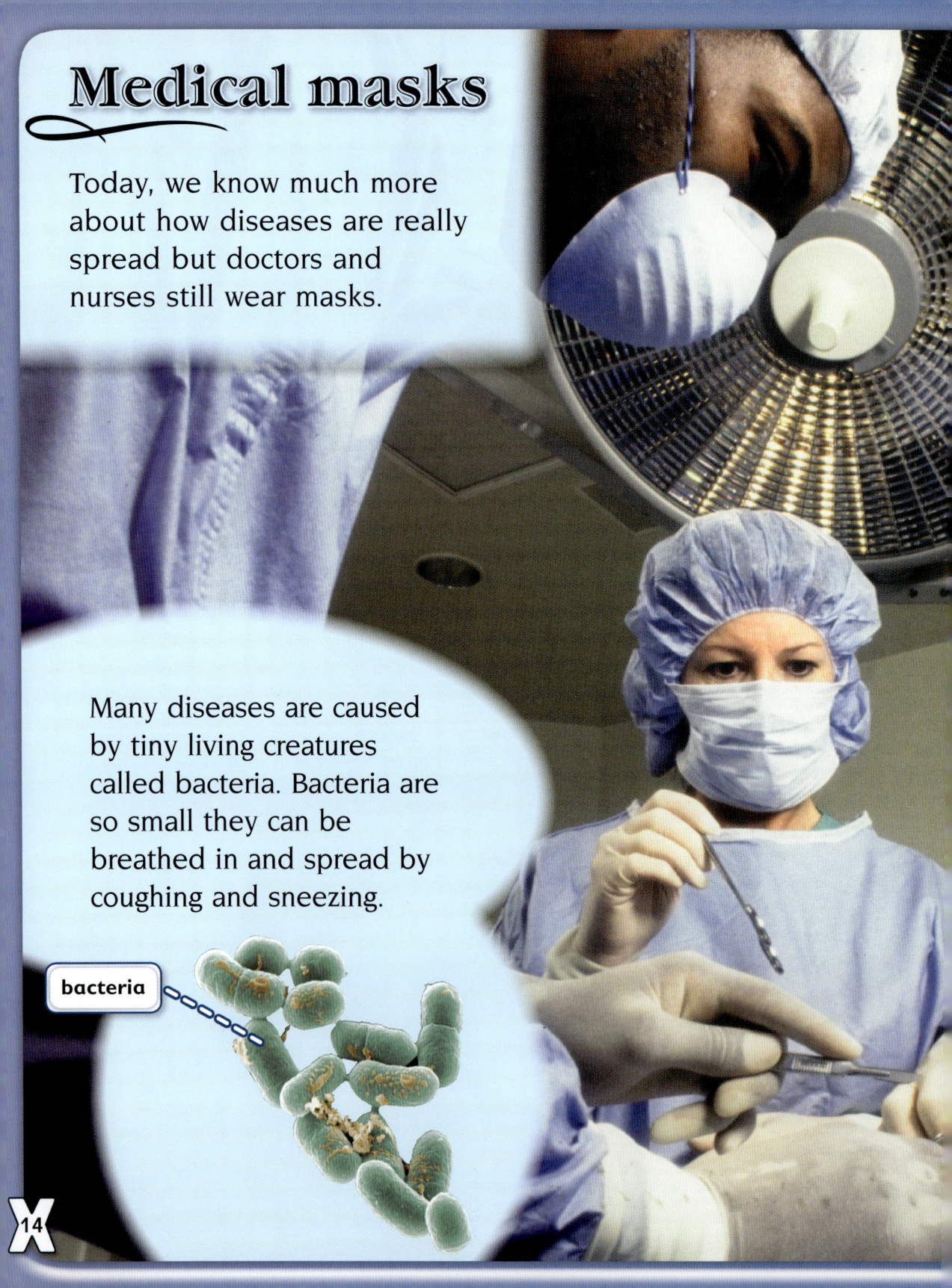

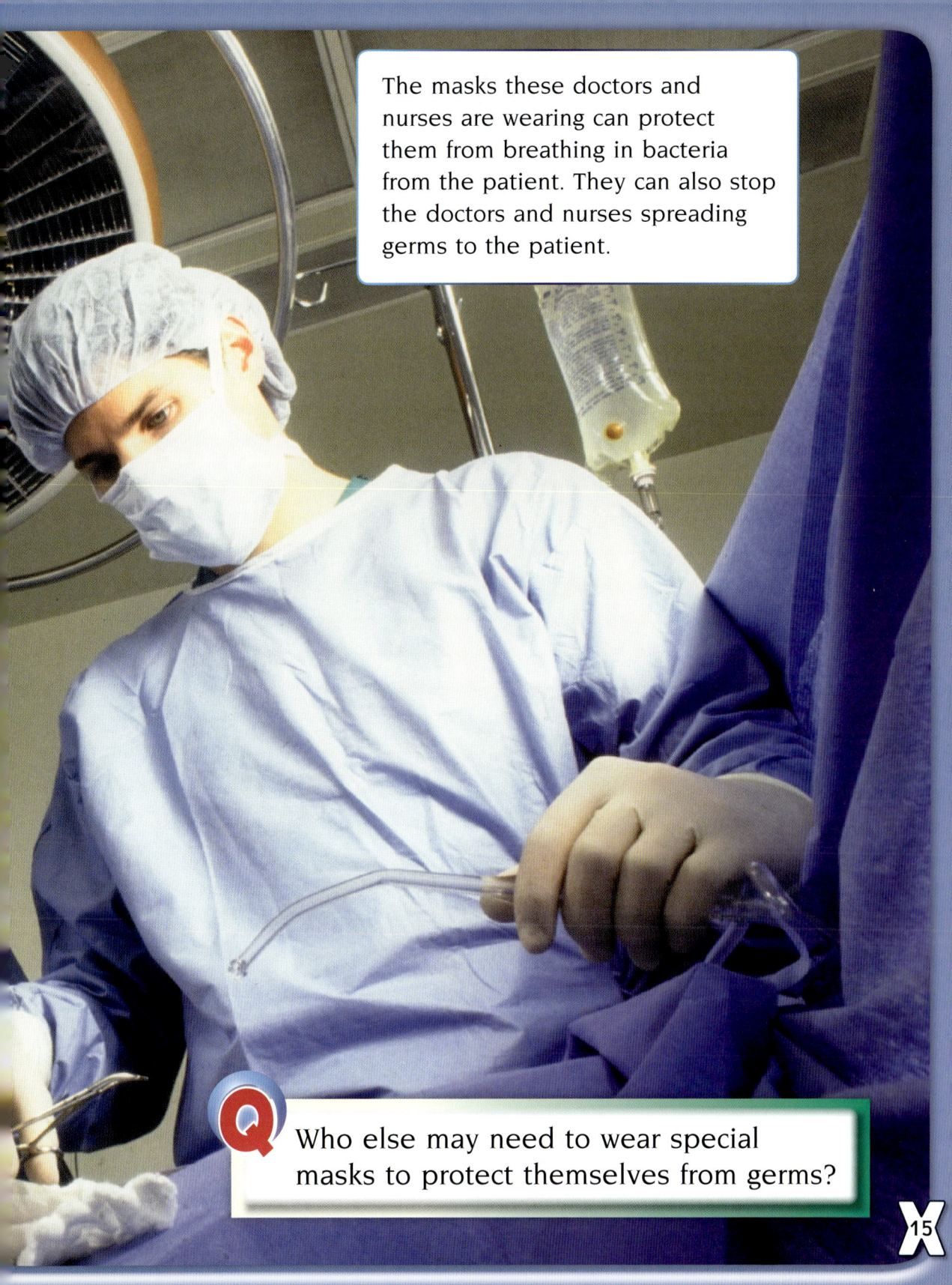

The masks these doctors and nurses are wearing can protect them from breathing in bacteria from the patient. They can also stop the doctors and nurses spreading germs to the patient.

Q Who else may need to wear special masks to protect themselves from germs?

Sporting masks

Sports can be great fun – and good for your health! Some sports can be dangerous. A lot of sportsmen and women need to wear a mask so they can play their favourite sport safely.

In cricket, some bowlers can bowl at more than 145km per hour! That's why batsmen wear helmets with a face guard – like knights going into battle!

Ice hockey players could get badly injured by other players' sticks if they didn't wear a mask.

Mask quiz

Q Can you guess what sport these masks and helmets are being used for? And can you tell from the mask what the danger is?
The answers are on page 24.

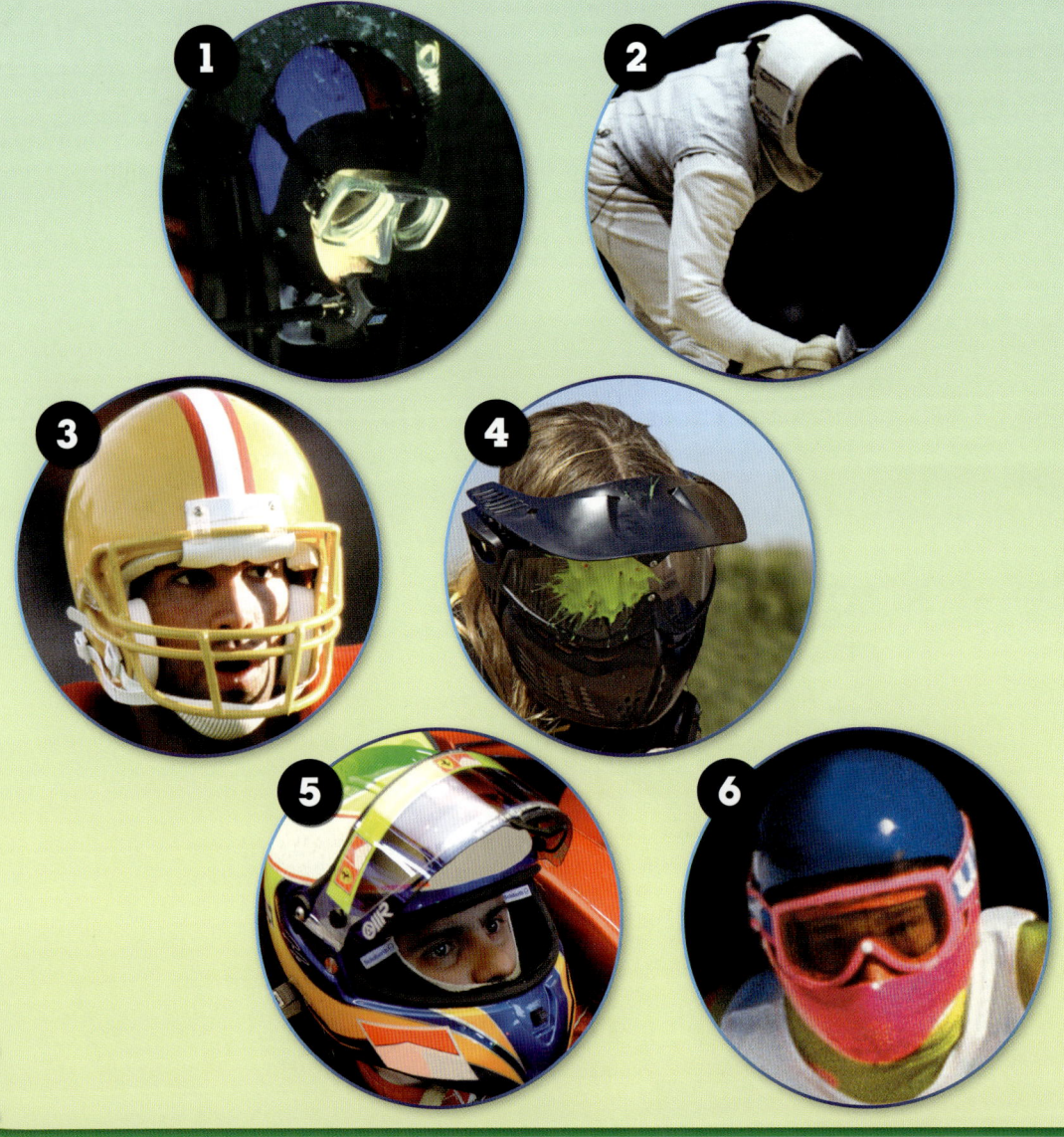

1

2

3

4

5

6

18

Masks at work

Police diver

This police diver wears a mask to let her breathe underwater. Unlike a sports diver, the police diver's mask covers her whole face. Police divers often have to work in dirty water with lots of germs. Their masks protect them from diseases too.

Welder

This man is joining two pieces of metal together. This is called welding. A welder needs a special mask to protect his eyes from the bright light and sparks.

Fire-fighter

Fire-fighters wear masks and helmets to protect their faces from the heat and flames of a fire.

Fire-fighters also wear special masks to help them breathe.

Heroes and villains

Robbers and bandits have worn masks so they can't be identified and caught.

Crime-fighters and superheroes in books and comics often wear masks, too.

In olden times, robbers wore masks when they robbed travellers on quiet roads.

Zorro
One of the first modern masked heroes was Zorro. Zorro protected poor people from rich bullying lords – even though Zorro was a rich man himself. Zorro means 'fox' in Spanish. He was too cunning to be caught.

Batman

Batman didn't have superpowers but he had lots of **gadgets** to help him fight crime, like his Batrope and Batmobile.

Spiderman

Spiderman is the secret super identity of Peter Parker. Spiderman has superpowers. He can climb like a spider and shoot out sticky webs from his hands.

If you could be a superhero or heroine, which super power would you have? What mask and costume would you **design** for yourself?

Glossary

armour   special clothes used in battle to keep a person safe

bomb   a weapon that explodes and hurts people or things

design   a plan for making or doing something

disease   an illness

filter   something used to get substances out of a liquid or gas

gadgets   useful things or tools

gas   a substance like air

germ   a tiny living thing that is hard to see. Some germs can make you ill

helmet   a strong hat used to keep your head safe

infect   to spread disease

jousting   a contest where two knights fight on horseback with long spears

knight   a person who wore armour and rode into battle on a horse

medieval   during the middle ages (a long time ago)

plague   a disease that spreads widely

shield   shaped piece of metal or wood used for protection

sign   1)signal 2) a mark of identification

symbol   a mark or sign

victim   someonewho has been hurt, robbed or killed

visor   piece on helmet that covers the face

Index

Answers to 'Mask' quiz on page 18:
1: Diving, the water; 2: Fencing, sword;
3: Football, football; 4: Paintballing, paintball;
5: Racing driving, a crash; 6: Skiing, snow and sun.